Napa Valley Mustard Festival Cookbook

Edited and Compiled

by

Susan J. Parker

© **1994**

Front Cover/Fine Art:

Sara Barnes

Back Cover/Fine Art & Poetry:

Anne Hunter Hamilton

Graphic Design: Dina Mande

Balsac Communications & Marketing

"The kingdom of heaven is like a grain of mustard seed, which a man took and sowed in his field. This indeed is the smallest of seeds; but when it grows up it is larger than any herb and becomes a tree, so that the birds of the air come and dwell in its branches."

Matthew Chapter 13, Verse 31

Napa Valley Mustard Festival
Logo Design by Jan Wiltsey Sofie

Napa Valley Mustard Festival

When the winter season blazes with wild mustard in bloom, splashing the valley with a sea of brilliant yellow, Napa Valley hosts the Napa Valley Mustard Festival. If you haven't seen mustard blooming in the vineyards of Napa Valley, you've missed on of the most beautiful sights on earth, according to George Rothwell and Susan Parker, primary forces behind the establishment of the Napa Valley Festival.

The two month festival is a valley wide joint promotional effort. The festival's purpose is to attract visitors to Napa Valley during this beautiful time of year and to enhance a variety of art and educational programs through festival activities.

The highlight of the festival is the Napa Valley Mustard Celebration hosted by Calistoga over Valentine's Day weekend. This event will offer a tasting of over 100 different mustards, as well as wine tastings, micro-brewery tasting, entertainment for all ages, gourmet food booths, and an art and craft exhibit. The recipes found in this book have been collected from Celebration participants.

The Napa Valley Mustard Festival has many events and activities including the poster design contest and silent auction, a Kodak sponsored Photography Contest, winemakers dinners, special restaurant menus, a golf tournament, culinary classes and demonstrations, and several dances. Napa Valley invites you to come experience the magic of the mustard! For more information on the Napa Valley Mustard Festival and a complete program guide call 800~4~YOUNTVILLE.

DEDICATION

This book is dedicated to the people who supported the inaugural year of the Napa Valley Mustard Festival. Those who contributed the necessary funding, time, expertise, and creativity to this project are indeed worthy of acknowledgment.

SPECIAL THANKS

To all the chefs and innkeepers who took the time to share their recipes with the mustard lovers of the world.

To Joanne Lockwood who typed and typed and typed until this cookbook was done.

To Calistoga Press for their patience and perseverance in printing this collection of recipes.

To Sylvia Scott for being one incredible human being.

To Alexi and Eric who supported Mom through the thick and the thin of Mustard Mania!

TABLE OF CONTENTS

The Aidells Sausage Company began February, 1983 as supplier to a handful of top-notch chefs in the San Francisco Bay Area. Over the years, Aidells Sausage Company has become nationally regarded by food writers, chefs, specialty food professionals and gourmands. Bruce's love of experimentation and appreciation of great flavors has continued throughout his career with sausages like Chicken and Turkey with Sun-Dried Tomatoes and Basil, New Mexico, Whiskey Fennel, and Lamb and Beef with Fresh Rosemary.

Real Beer and Good Eats (The Rebirth of America's Beer and Food Traditions) is Bruce Aidells' most recent cookbook, published by Alfred A. Knopf. Aidells also wrote *Hot Links and Country Flavors* which received the IACP *"Best Single Subject"* Cookbook Award.

Aidells' Porter Pot Roast

4-5 lb.	Chuck roast, bottom round or rump roast, (boned and tied)
3 tbsp.	olive oil
2 lb.	onions, peeled, halved, & thinly sliced
1	carrot, diced
1	rib celery, diced
6	garlic cloves, chopped
1 tbsp.	molasses
4	bay leaves
2 ~ 12oz.	bottles Porter or other dale ale or beer
2 tbsp.	Dijon or coarse-grained mustard
1 tbsp.	malt or red wine vinegar, or to taste
1 lb.	Aidells Hunter's, Andouille or Hot Bier Sausage, sliced

Season the meat generously with salt and pepper, thyme, and sage. In a heavy Dutch oven or casserole large enough to hold the meat, heat the oil over medium-high heat. Put in the roast, and sear it on all sides. Remove the roast, and add the onions, carrot, celery, garlic and molasses. Cover and cook over medium heat for about 10-12 minutes, until the onions are soft and beginning to color. Put the meat back in with the bay leaves and beer. Cover and cook for 1-1/2 - 2 hours over low heat until the meat is tender.

Add sausage and cook 10 minutes more. Remove the meat and keep it warm. Degrease the liquid in the pot, and stir in the mustard and the vinegar. Boil the sauce until it just becomes syrupy. Taste for salt and pepper and vinegar. Slice the roast. Pour some of the sauce and vegetables over the meat and serve. Pass the rest of the sauce separately. Serves 6-8.

Aidells Roasted Lamb Sausage with Mustard-Rosemary Glaze

1/2 C.	smooth Dijon mustard
1 tbsp.	soy sauce
2 tsp.	minced garlic
2 tsp.	chopped fresh rosemary
2 tbsp.	fruity olive oil
1 ~ 4 lb.	Lamb, Rosemary and Mustard Sausage in one piece, coiled

Mix together the mustard, soy sauce, garlic, and rosemary. Gradually whisk in the olive oil until it is absorbed into the sauce. Preheat the oven to 375 degrees. Place the sausage coiled in a roasting pan. Brush generously will all the glaze and roast for 30 minutes, or until the glaze begins to brown and the sausage is firm and cooked through.

ROSEMARY

Aidells Asparagus Wrapped in Country Ham in Mustard Vinaigrette

1 lb.	large asparagus trimmed
1/2 lb.	thinly sliced country Smithfield or Westphalian Ham
1 tbsp.	Dijon mustard
1 tbsp.	chopped shallots
1/2 tsp.	minced garlic
2 tbsp.	chopped fresh parsley
2 tbsp.	red wine vinegar
6 tbsp.	olive oil

Steam or boil the asparagus until tender about 6 minutes. Let cool and wrap the crisp spears in slices of the ham. Arrange on a platter.

In a food processor or mixing bowl mix together the mustard, shallots, garlic, parsley, and vinegar. Gradually blend in the olive oil.

Pour dressing over the wrapped asparagus spears, and serve.

ALL SEASONS
CAFE & CATERING

All Seasons Cafe & Catering features food "...as fresh and sparkling as the California countryside. The food is inventive and intensely flavored," says the San Francisco Chronicle. Menus draw inspiration from the wealth of the North Coast and locally grown products and are arranged to complement the many fine wines and fine Pinot Noir and Chardonnay from California, Oregon and France. The expertise and knowledge of local wine and food extend to off premise locations in event catering. Services range from gala weddings to wine tastings to rustic country picnics.

All Seasons was founded in 1983 and is owned and operated by Alex and Mark Dierkhising and Gayle Keller who have also owned the Silverado Restaurant in Calistoga since 1976. Both establishments are nationally known for their outstanding wine lists. Mark Dierkhising, executive chef, studied with Madeleine Kamman at the School for American Chefs and graduated from the Culinary Institute of America.

All Seasons Cafe & Catering
Sauteed Field Mushrooms
With Deep Fried Leeks

4 oz.	sweet butter
2	shallots, chopped
2	cloves garlic, chopped
4 tbsp.	chopped parsley
2 tbsp.	chopped tarragon
1 tbsp.	chopped sage
1 lb.	wild mushrooms
1 pt.	chicken stock
1 C.	heavy cream
4 tbsp.	dijon mustard
2	leeks
1/4 C.	all purpose flour
1 qt.	vegetable oil
	salt and pepper

Julienne leeks and place in a bowl of cold water to clean. Pull leeks out of water using your fingers, leaving dirt behind. Dry in paper towels and sprinkle with flour. Heat oil to 350 degrees in large pot. Fry leeks in oil. Remove when brown and drain on paper towels. Set aside.

Clean and slice mushrooms. In large saute pan add butter, shallots, garlic and herbs. Saute until shallots are transparent. Add mushrooms and continue to cook for one minute. Add stock, cream and mustard. Reduce by half or more. Add salt and pepper to taste. Divide onto four plates and garnish with leeks.

All Seasons Cafe & Catering
Smoked Chicken Penne Pasta

12 oz	shredded smoked chicken
4 oz	extra virgin olive oil
1 tbsp.	chopped garlic
2 tbsp.	chopped parsley
1 tsp.	chopped tarragon
1 tsp.	chopped sage
4 tbsp.	diced black olives
4 tbsp.	minced sundried tomatoes
2 tbsp.	dijon mustard
20 oz.	cooked penne pasta
4 oz.	shredded romano cheese
	salt and pepper to taste

Preheat a large stainless steel saute pan over a high heat. Remove pan from heat and add olive oil, shallots, garlic, parsley, tarragon, sage and black olives. Place over high heat and saute one to two minutes. Add sundried tomatoes, dijon mustard, chicken broth, and smoked chicken. Cook till the liquid is reduced by half. Add pasta to pan and heat through, season with salt and pepper. Divide among four plates and serve garnished with Romano cheese.

Situated high on Rutherford Hill, Auberge Du Soleil, a romantic country restaurant and hideaway, is nestled in an olive grove overlooking the lovely Napa Valley. Cedar columns, rough timbered ceiling, a magnificent fireplace, pink table linens and fresh flowers create a warm rustic ambience. Light classical music plays in a room that opens out to a wisteria-decked, umbrella-topped terrace with a panoramic view of the valley below.

The Auberge is the epitome of gracious, fine dining and a stunning setting for Chef David Hale's classic Wine Country Cuisine. Breakfast, lunch and dinner are served in the fashionable dining room or Al fresco on the terrace. The menu changes often, and always features tasty, elegantly presented delicacies such as roasted lobster sausage with citrus-mustard vinaigrette and ancho-mustard glazed pork chop on horseradish whipped potatoes. The Auberge is one of the truly luxurious and romantic spots from which to explore the beautiful Napa Valley.

Auberge du Soleil
Warm Peach-Mustard Compote

1	small onion, diced
3	whole ripe peaches, peeled and diced
1 tbsp.	maple syrup
4 oz.	mild brown mustard
2 tbsp.	cracked black pepper

Sweat onion in butter over medium heat until tender and translucent (approximately 5 minutes). Remove from heat. Add diced peaches and maple syrup. Toss gently. Transfer mixture into medium mixing bowl. Fold in mustard, parsley and cracked pepper. Hold in refrigerator for at least 4 hours. Serve with baked ham or grilled meats and sausages.

BIG DADDY'S
at the
Calistoga Gliderport

Take a step back into the 50's at Big Daddy's Restaurant at the Calistoga Gliderport, enjoy music of the times, the flavor of 100% Harris Ranch ground beef burgers, and the sight of gliders soaring silently above town. Saturday Classic Car Night at Big Daddy's returns in May. Thirty-plus classic cars will carry you away as you remember special cars and forgotten times. Bring your own classic, or stop by to vote on your favorite classic car. Each Saturday night winner gets a glider ride for two.

Big Daddy's is rapidly developing the reputation for the best hamburgers and oven roasted turkey sandwiches in the Napa Valley. Big Daddy's is also known for its real milk shakes and malts using Lappert's Hawaiian Ice Cream. Children will enjoy several menu items for the smaller appetites between rides on the carousel next to the sand filled playground.

Big Daddy's Hamburgers

5 oz.	100% pure Harris Ranch ground beef
1 tbsp.	Lawry's Seasoned Salt
2 tbsp.	mayonnaise
1 tsp.	yellow mustard
1 tsp.	whole grain dijon mustard
	lettuce, tomato and red onion
	(dill pickle on the side)
	sesame seed bun
	canola oil

Mix 2 tbsp. of mayonnaise, 1 tsp. of yellow mustard and 1 tsp. of whole grain dijon mustard and set aside. Shape ground beef into patty. Combine 1 tbsp. Lawry's Seasoned Salt and 1 tsp. of Steak Shake. Place patty on grill at medium heat and sprinkle with seasoning mixture. Cook 3-4 minutes, turn, and again add seasoning.

Oil bun and place on grill for 3-4 minutes or until toasted to your taste. Remove bun and add mustard sauce to both halves of the bun. Add desired vegetables, placing onion on bottom half of bun (the onion will stay there and not float around on top of the hamburger). Remove hamburger when cooked to your taste.

Just north of St. Helena the wine country traveler will find Brava Terrace - the creation of chef/owner Fred Halpert. Inspired by the wine country cooking of France, Italy and California, Chef Halpert and Chef Peter McCaffrey have created a light style that relies heavily on fresh herbs, garlic, tomatoes, olive oil, and seafood. This combination is what these two chefs call, "cuisine of the sun."

As in its namesake, Brava Terrace boasts a lush, outdoor terrace providing priceless views of the Napa Valley landscape. Dining on the deck, guests overlook the restaurant's organic garden full of exotic peppers, herbs and tomatoes. Inside, the dining room is light and airy, with a whitewashed high ceiling and open kitchen. A dynamite wine list, seasonal and regional cooking, and a glorious setting add up to an impressive Napa Valley experience. Brava Terrace serves lunch and dinner continuously from 12:00 to 9:00. They are closed Wednesdays from November to April.

Brava Terrace
Seared Ahi Tuna Served Rare, Napa Valley Organic Greens, and a Tomato Mustard Seed Oil Vinaigrette

4	whole tomatoes
2 C.	mustard seed oil
1 tbsp.	fennel seeds
3 tbsp.	lemon juice
1 1/2 tbsp.	warm water
24 oz.	Ahi Tuna loin
12 oz.	mixed greens (red & green leaf, Boston, etc.)
1/4 C.	peanut oil
	salt and white pepper

Cut tops off tomatoes, then quarter and place in heavy sauce pot with 1 C. of mustard seed oil, and fennel seeds. Cook slowly over medium flame. Stir occasionally, after 15 minutes the tomatoes will start to break down. Remove from heat and let cool. Place tomatoe mixture in food processor, puree mixture, then slowly add the remaining mustard oil, then lemon juice and water. Season to taste with salt and pepper.

Prepare green leaf, red leaf, Boston lettuce, etc. for use in salad, tearing into bite size pieces. Wash salad and dry.

Cut tuna into 2 oz. portions, dredge through the peanut oil. Season with salt and pepper. Sear the tuna rare, over hot grill or with a hot skillet.

Toss the greens with a small amount of the vinaigrette, set the greens on the plate, then place the tuna on the greens. Garnish with a small amount of the mustard vinaigrette and serve.

CALISTOGA INN

Calistoga Inn is an establishment with a rich history, like the town whose name it shares. As long as Calistoga's hot springs and mudbaths have been drawing folks to town, the Calistoga Inn & Restaurant has always been a favored place to stay, not to mention a flavorful place to dine. Breakfast, lunch or dinner, the Inn does delicious justice to them all, with a marvelous combination of regional dishes, with special attention to fresh fish and good old American barbecue. Of course, to wash it all down, the Calistoga Inn offers its own homemade brews: Golden Lager, Wheat Ale and Red Ale.

So when you come to Calistoga, wander down to the Inn at the end of town, down by the river. We offer 18 charming B&B rooms with shared bath, all with comfy double beds, and with only a one-night minimum stay. Come enjoy the Calistoga Inn & Restaurant and the Napa Valley Brewing Company.

Calistoga Inn
Napa Wings In
Sweet-Sour Mustard Sauce

1 pkg.	chicken wings
1 C.	Sweet Thai Chilli Sauce
2 tbsp.	whole grain mustard
2 tbsp.	ketchup
2 tbsp.	BBQ sauce
1	clove chopped garlic
	parsley, chopped
	tobasco to taste

Combine all ingredients and toss with wings. Roast in 350 degree oven turning frequently until done. Or deep fry wings dusted with flour and toss with sauce. Serve with celery and Ranch Dressing for dip.

Built in 1929, the Candlelight Inn is a lovely English Tudor in a serene one-acre, parklike setting. Most rooms have private balconies, decks, large two-person marble jacuzzi baths and marble fireplaces in the bedrooms for a romantic evening. All rooms have private baths, TVs, telephones and views overlooking the gardens or rolling hills.

Special features range from a beautiful courtyard garden, cathedral ceilings, antiques and stained-glass window to four-poster beds and private saunas. Start the day with an exquisite candlelight breakfast served in the beautiful Victorian breakfast room and end by a refreshing dip in the pool. Close to Napa Valley Wine Train and wineries.

Candlelight Inn
Turkey Crisps

1/3 C.	olive oil
3 tbsp.	lemon juice
	salt
8 1/4 lb.	slices of turkey breast
4 tsp.	dijon mustard
2	eggs
3 C.	soft bread crumbs
2 tbsp.	butter
	parsley, chopped and lemon wedges for garnish

Mix 2 tbsp. of the oil with the lemon juice and a pinch of salt in a shallow dish. Add the turkey. Mix well and leave to marinate for 1 hour.

Drain the turkey and pat dry on paper towels. Spread thinly with the mustard. Beat the eggs lightly on a plate and use to coat turkey. Dip the turkey slices into the bread crumbs, pressing gently.

Melt the butter and remaining oil in a skillet and gently fry the turkey for about 10 minutes on each side, till tender and golden.

Drain on paper towels and arrange on a warmed dish. Garnish with chopped parsley, lemon wedges and serve immediately with a tomato and onion salad dressed with vinaigrette.

Since opening in 1987, Checkers restaurant has established itself as a favorite spot for locals to get a delicious, reasonably priced meal. The decor is upbeat, relaxed, and inviting with hardwood floors, high ceiling, and comtemporary art gracing the walls.

For breakfast, patrons enjoy macadamian nut waffles, andouille sausage omelets as well as standard breakfast fare. The lunch/dinner menu has mouth watering salads, pizzas and pastas to offer such as the blackened chicken Caesar salad; the procuitto, mushroom and smoked mozzarella pizza or a firecracker chicken pasta. Also known for the best frozen yogurt bar in the valley. A fine selection of local wines and beers compliment the diverse menu. An emphasis on fresh, healthy ingredients makes Checkers a preferred choice for dining in Calistoga.

Checkers
Napa Valley Salad with
Dijon Mustard Dressing

1/2 C.	white wine vinegar
1/4 C.	sugar
1/3 C.	dijon mustard
	pinch of salt and pepper
2/3 C.	salad oil
1 tbsp.	poppy seeds
	mixed greens
	toasted walnuts, chopped
	cubed apples
	crumbled gorgonzola cheese
	raisins

Combine vinegar, sugar, dijon mustard, salt and pepper. Mix well, slowly pour oil into mixture and emulsify. Add poppy seeds.

Wash and dry desired amount of greens. Toss with enough dressing to coat. Sprinkle cheese, chopped nuts, apples and raisins.

Cinnamon Bear
Bed & Breakfast

A classic Arts and Crafts, the Metzner House was built in 1904 and given as a wedding gift to Susan Smith from her father when she married Walter Metzner. Her husband later became Mayor of St. Helena for 20 years. Genny Jenkins bought the house from the Metzner estate to raise her three children. When the youngest left for college, she began renting rooms to overnight guests visiting the wineries. The Cinnamon Bear name developed from her oldest son's affection for a stuffed bear named Oliver who saw him through tough exams at Stanford University. Suddenly, stuffed bears started filling the house and entertaining the guests with all sorts of "unbearable" pranks.

The home is furnished in the style of the 1920's with many fine antiques. Gleaming hardwood floors and oriental carpets add to its unique elegance. Central air conditioning, private bathrooms and queen-size beds in all four rooms provide guests with all the comforts.

Cinnamon Bear
Bed & Breakfast
"Bearly" Benedict

8	eggs
3/4 C.	cream
1 tsp.	dry mustard
	salt, pepper, dill (to taste)
4 - 5	english muffins
8-10	canadian bacon slices
1 1/2 C.	hollandaise sauce

Blend eggs, cream, mustard, and seasonings. Scramble in pan. Split english muffins and butter, place under broiler till toasted. Heat slices of canadian bacon in sauce pan. Use commercial package of hollandaise or your favorite recipe. Assemble Benedict on large platter: muffin, canadian bacon, scambled egg mixture, and hollandaise sauce. Garnish with paprika and mustard greens.

**EAST SHORE
SPECIALTY
FOODS**

*established with pride,
in 1986*

East Shore Specialty Foods was first developed from original recipes in the kitchen of the home pictured on their label, located on the East Shore of a small Wisconsin lake.

Today, production takes place in a custom designed commercial kitchen in Nashotah (No-sho-tah), Wisconsin. While output has increased significantly, the original recipes and the small batch process has remained. East Shore mustards and pretzels are mixed and seasoned by hand to insure the quality, texture and distinct taste.

Since the introduction of their original Sweet and Tangy Mustard in 1986, they've added two new mustards, "Coarse with Dill" and "Mild with Tarragon". They also make two kinds of seasoned pretzels. All of their products share the same high quality standards.

East Shore Specialty Foods
Barb's Mustard-Grilled
Chicken Breasts

1	medium close garlic
1	onion , quartered
1/4 C.	parsley sprigs
1/4 C.	East Shore Sweet & Tangy Mustard
1/4 C.	lemon juice
1/4 C.	olive oil
1 tsp.	worcestershire sauce
4	whole boneless chicken breasts, skinned and halved

In food processor, mince garlic. Add onion and parsley, coarsely chop. Add mustard, lemon juice, oil, worcestershire, 1/2 tsp. salt with 1/4 tsp. pepper; puree. In shallow baking dish, cover chicken with garlic mixture. Refrigerate 2 hours.

Prepare outdoor grill for barbecue. Drain chicken, reserving marinade. Grill (or broil) chicken 5 minutes on each side, or until cooked through. In saucepan, simmer marinade 5 minutes; serve with chicken breasts.

East Shore Specialty Foods
Ruth Ann's Pommes de Terre

6-8	medium - large baking potatoes
1/4 lb.	melted butter or margarine
3 tbsp.	East Shore Coarse with Dill Mustard
	salt and pepper to taste

Select a 9" pan, about 2 1/2" deep, butter well.

Clean and slice potatoes thinly. Blend butter and East Shore Coarse with Dill Mustard. Add to sliced potatoes and toss to coat evenly.

Arrange the slices around the pan and cover the bottom, overlapping the slices. Sprinkle with salt and pepper. Continue to build up layers - filling the pan. If any butter and mustard remains, pour over the top. Press the potatoes down so that pan is filled evenly.

Bake in 400 degree oven until slices are tender. They will brown on the top - 40-45 minutes.

Remove from oven and let stand a couple of minutes. Run a sharp knife around the edge of the pan. Invert and unmold onto a serving plate.

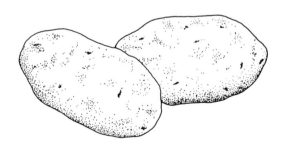

East Shore Specialty Foods
Joy's Mushroom Mustard Soup

1/4 C.	butter
4	whole green onions, thinly sliced
2 lb.	fresh mushrooms, thinly sliced
6 C.	chicken stock
1 tbsp.	fresh chopped parsley
1/2 C.	dry sherry
1/4 C.	East Shore Sweet & Tangy Mustard
	freshly ground pepper
1 C.	half and half

Melt butter in heavy, large saucepan over medium heat and cook until lightly browned. Add mushrooms and onions. Saute until liquid evaporates, stirring often. Add stock, sherry, parsley and East Shore Sweet & Tangy Mustard. Simmer ten minutes. Season with pepper. Add cream and warm through. Serve immediately.

Foothill House

Tucked among the gently rolling vineyards, wineries, and a town known for its mineral pools and mud baths, rests the Foothill House Bed and Breakfast.

The Inn is surrounded by a variety of lovely old trees and beautiful shrubbery. Each spacious guest suite is individually decorated with country antiques and four poster beds. All have private entrances and baths, small refrigerators and fireplaces. A luxurious private cottage with a two sided fireplace, Jacuzzi tub and secluded patio provide a perfect setting for lovers.

Attention to detail is a priority of innkeepers, Doris and Gus Beckert. Doris, a former student at the California Culinary Academy, has a flair for food, both from a taste and presentation standpoint. Gourmet breakfasts and evening hors'dourvres reflect her talents. The Beckerts pride themselves in helping guests plan their stay.

Foothill House
Salad with Mustard Dressing

1/2	small onion, chopped
3 tbsp.	cider vinegar
2 tsp.	spicy brown mustard
1/2 tsp.	sugar
1/2 tsp.	salt
1/4 tsp.	ground pepper
1 C.	vegetable oil
1/2 lb.	bacon
2	bunches romaine lettuce
2 ~ 8.5oz	cans water packed artichokes, drained and quartered
4 oz.	blue cheese, crumbled cherry tomatoes, optional

Dressing: Puree onion and vinegar in food processor, add mustard, sugar , salt and pepper. Gradually add oil in a thin steady stream and continue blending until thick.

Salad: cook bacon until crisp - drain on paper towels and crumble. Tear romaine into bite size pieces. Place in salad bowl and add crumbled bacon, artichoke hearts, blue cheese, crumbled, cherry tomatoes. Toss with dressing to taste and serve.

Foothill House
Garlic Filet of Beef with
Mustard Sauce

2 1/2 lb.	Beef tenderloin roast
2 tbsp.	olive oil
1 tbsp.	unsalted butter
4	shallots, minced
2 C.	beef stock
2 tbsp.	cognac
2 tbsp.	dijon mustard
3 tbsp .	fresh parsley , minced
1/2 C.	butter, cut into 8 pieces
	garlic, sliced
	salt and pepper

Heat oven to 450 degrees. Every 3/4 " slice roast 1/2" down and insert slices of garlic. Brush roast with oil. Heat 2 tbsp. oil in skillet over medium heat and add meat. Brown and roast meat for 30 minutes at 350 degrees for rare meat.

Sauce: Use same skillet you browned the meat in and add shallots and stir in stock. Scrape any brown bits into stock. Reduce stock in half , add cognac - boil 1 minute, reduce heat, stir in mustard, parsley and whisk in butter 1 piece at a time - season with salt and pepper. Serve sauce on the side of roast.

Forest Manor

Steeped in splendid solitude and nestled in a vast glade of evergreens and vineyards above the Napa Valley floor, this 20 acre English Tudor estate reflects the magic of Napa's Wine Country. The three story manor is tastefully furnished with English antiques, Persian carpets and oriental artifacts. The romantic ambiance is enhanced with massive hand hewn beams, high vaulted ceilings and large windows overlooking the wooded landscape. Guests especially enjoy the 53 foot pool and spa, decks, secluded setting, and peaceful strolls through the surrounding forests and picturesque vineyards.

Three spacious suites with private baths, queen or king beds, in-room refrigerators, coffee makers, robes, some with fireplaces and verandas, and one with private jacuzzi. Guests enjoy freshly baked cookies, complimentary hot and soft drinks, breakfast served in the dining room, on the veranda or in their suites.

Forest Manor
Asparagus Tomato Quiche

1	10" pie shell, partially baked
4 lg.	eggs
3 tbsp.	flour
1 tsp.	paprika
1 tsp.	salt
1/2 tsp.	dry mustard
1 1/2 C.	half-and-half
2 C.	grated swiss cheese
10	fresh asparagus spears
1 med.	tomato, sliced in 4 or 6 slices

Preheat oven to 375 degrees. Beat eggs with next 5 ingredients. Stir in cheese. Saving 4 or 6 asparagus spears for the top, chop the rest into 1" lengths, lay on bottom of pie shell. Pour in liquid. Bake 20 minutes. Remove and quickly arrange tomato and asparagus on top in a wagon wheel pattern. Bake another 20-30 minutes.

HENNESSEY HOUSE

Hennessey House is a Queen Anne Victorian house built in 1889 and listed on the National Register of Historic Places. The inn was recently repainted in five colors, with gold leaf highlighting some of the unique architectural features. Hennessey House offers ten beautifully appointed guestrooms, all with private baths and furnished in antiques. The carriage house rooms feature two-person whirlpool tubs and antique vanities with double sinks. Selected rooms have fireplaces, feather beds or canopy beds.

A full gourmet breakfast is served in the dining room which is known for its unique hand-painted, stamped, tin ceiling original with the house. Guests can relax in the comfortable parlor which offers a wood-burning fireplace as well as books, games and a television. Complimentary sherry is offered in the guestrooms. On Friday and Saturday night guests can enjoy wine and hor d'oeuvres while meeting other guests.

Hennessey House
Sausage Cheese Strata

3 C.	croutons with Italian spices
3 tbsp.	melted butter
1 C.	shredded monterey jack cheese (w/pesto or garlic spices)
1 C.	shredded swiss cheese
1 lb.	sausage
10	eggs
1-1/4 C.	milk
1/4 C.	chopped green onions
2 tbsp.	mustard
1/4 C.	dry white wine
1~ 10 3/4oz	can cream of celery or cream of mushroom soup

Lightly butter 9x13 baking dish. Spread out croutons. Sprinkle melted butter. Top with monterey jack and swiss cheeses. Cook sausage, drain, crumble onto cheeses.

Beat eggs, milk, chopped green onions, mustard, wine, soup and mustard. Pour over sausage, cheese, crouton layers. Cover with foil and refrigerate over night. Let stand at room temperature for 30 minutes. Baked covered for 30 minutes at 350 degrees, bake uncovered 30 minutes. Let stand 5 minutes before slicing into 10 squares.

La chaumière
a country inn

An abundance of flowers greet you as you walk up the entrance to La Chaumiére, located across from a city park and 1/2 block from downtown shops, spas and restaurants. Two rooms are done in french Victorian furniture with full baths and queen-sized beds. One offers a private sitting room; and the other, french doors leading onto a private deck. You can relax under a tree house, next to a 950 sq. ft. log cabin, with living room, kitchen, bath and bedroom with king-size bed.

Wine and cheese are served in the afternoon; port or sherry in the rooms for a nightcap, and a full 2 course gourmet breakfast in the morning. The innkeeper, Gary Venturi, makes sure your stay is comfortable, pleasing and memorable. The inn is small, so conscious thought is given to your needs on an individual basis, and care is taken to see that your visit to the Napa Valley wine country and Calistoga are complete.

La Chaumiére Bed & Breakfast
Baked Italian Sausage Frittata

1 1/2 lb.	mild Italian bulk sausage
1/2-3/4lb.	fresh mushrooms, sliced
2 tbsp.	butter or margarine
	garlic powder
1/4 C.	white wine
3 lg.	swiss chard leaves, rolled and sliced thin
9 lg.	eggs
1-1/4C.	milk
2 tbsp.	dijon mustard

In skillet brown and drain sausage; spread evenly over bottom of 9x13" baking dish. Saute mushrooms in butter and wine until almost all liquid is absorbed. Spread mushrooms over sausage. Next, layer the swiss chard and cheese. In a bowl beat the eggs, milk and dijon mustard and pour evenly over all.

Place in preheated 350 degree oven on middle rack. Bake 1 hour, uncovered. Remove from oven, and let stand 10-15 minutes. Divide and cut into 8 squares. Serve with a dollop of sour cream on top and chopped chives or greens from green onions. Also, good with salsa. Country Style Potatoes with Bell peppers, onions and Italian Seasonings is a good side dish.

La Chaumiére Bed & Breakfast
Salad Dressing

2 med.	tomatoes (blanched and skins removed)
1/2 C.	vegetable oil
1/2 C.	olive oil
1/4 C.	vinegar
1/2 C.	lemon juice
1 tbsp.	pesto
2 tbsp.	dijon mustard
3	cloves garlic
	salt and pepper to taste

Blend all the above ingredients in a food processor or blender until smooth. Will keep 1-2 weeks in refrigerator.

Lord Derby Arms
English Pub and Restaurant

The Lord Derby Arms English Pub & Restaurant has been established in Calistoga since 1984. A unique country pub situated at the end of the Silverado Trail in the Napa Valley. They specialize in all the traditional English pub fare such as fish-n-chips, bangers and mash, Shepherd's pie, and much more. Their vast selection of beers and ales on tap are rivaled by none, Harp lager, Guiness stout and Bass ale, to name a few. And no English pub is complete without the traditional dartboard in the bar.

Outdoor dining on the deck overlooks vineyards for those warm sunny days. A roaring fire inside the dining room warms guests on those cold, wintery nights. The Lord Derby Arms English Pub & Restaurant is located on the corner of Highway 29 and the Silverado Trail just outside of downtown Calistoga.

Lord Derby Arms
English Pub & Restaurant
Cornish Pasties

Pastry: 1 lb.   flour
                        salt, pinch
          8 oz.   butter
                        water to mix

Filling: 1 lb.   rump steak
          2 med.   potatoes
          2 med.   onions
          2   carrots
          2 tbsp.   stock or water and seasonings

Glaze: 1   egg, beaten

Dice the meat, potatoes, onions and carrots into small pieces. Mix with the stock or water and seasonings. Set aside.

Sift flour and salt. Rub in the butter. Bind to a rolling consistency with the water. Salt, pepper, thyme and bay leaves are good seasonings to use. Roll out the pastry, cut around 4 saucers.

Put the filling in the center of each round of pastry. Damp the edges of the pastry with water and bring the 2 halves together. Flute the edges with your fingers. Put them on a baking tray and brush with a beaten egg mixed with 2 tbsp. water. Bake for approximately 15 to 20 minutes in a 425 degree oven or until pastry is golden, then lower heat to 350 degrees and cook for 25-30 minutes more.

Mendocino Mustard has been hand-prepared in small batches on the Mendocino Coast of California since 1977. One of the very first gourmet mustards, it helped launch the current mustard mania.

This zesty, no-sodium mustard has long been favored as an extraordinary condiment and a cook's delight. Mendocino Mustard gets volumes of fan letters, declaiming "..simply the best mustard, I ever tasted", "..the most delicious I've ever had", "..we're addicted!".

Professional chefs, too, have made this mustard a must-have. Restaurants from the Cafe Beaujolais in Mendocino, to the New Otani Hotel in Los Angeles, to the Outrigger Prince Kuhio in Honolulu find Mendocino Mustard an invaluable addition to their menus. An excellent glaze for ham or fowl, it adds a zing to salad dressings, gravies and sauces, and elevates a sandwich to the sublime.

Mendocino Mustard
Spicy Creamy Dip

1 C.	cottage cheese (small curd)
1/2 C.	plain yogurt
1/2 C.	Mendocino Mustard
1 tsp.	chives, chopped
1 tsp.	shallots, minced
1 tsp.	fresh dill, chopped (or 1/4 tsp. dried dill)
1/2 tsp.	lemon juice

Whip cottage cheese in a blender or food processor until smooth. Add remaining ingredients, and stir just to blend. Dip with fresh vegetables or dried tomatoes. (Use lowfat cottage cheese and non-fat yogurt to make a very low fat, low calorie dip).

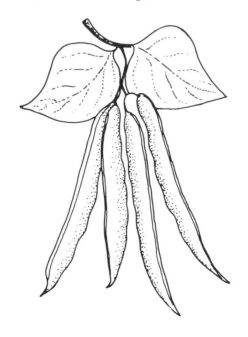

Mendocino Mustard
Colonel Mustard's Chicken

3 1/2-4 lb.	chicken, cut-up fryer
1/2 C.	dry bread crumbs
1/2 C.	Mendocino Mustard
2	cloves garlic, minced
2 tbsp.	olive oil
1/4 C.	minced parsley

Preheat oven to 350 degrees. Remove skin from chicken pieces and discard. Pat chicken dry with paper towels. Arrange in a single layer in a buttered baking dish. Coat chicken pieces with Mendocino Mustard, using a knife or spoon. Combine crumbs with garlic, olive oil and parsley. Pat the crumb mixture on the chicken pieces. Place chicken in oven and roast for 45 minutes. Remove from pan and serve.

The Mount Horeb Mustard Museum

The Mount Horeb Mustard Museum offers a dazzling selection of mustards, mustard making supplies, mustard books, and mustard memorabilia. Condimentally correct t-shirts, proclaim: "Mustard Happens!" For the true mustard aficionado, the Museum catalog offers mustard gift boxes for all occasions. Not to be missed is *The Proper Mustard*, the world's only mustard newsletter ("yellow journalism at its best.")

The Mustard Museum is located in beautiful south central Wisconsin, twenty miles from Madison, and is open year round, seven days a week. You can watch an informative video ("Mustardpiece Theatre"), feast your eyes on the world's largest collection of mustards (nearly 1,800 different varieties), and sample hundreds of unusual mustards.

Mount Horeb Mustard Museum
Mustard Butter Pasta

1 lb.	green pasta (fettucine)
7 tbsp.	soft butter
3 tbsp.	strong dijon mustard
3	shallots, minced
2	garlic cloves, minced
2 tsp.	balsamic vinegar
2 tbsp.	parsley, chopped
1 C.	bread crumbs
2	sundried tomatoes, minced
3-4 C.	broccoli and cauliflower florets, broken into small pieces
1	thin strip lemon peel, finely minced
	parmesan cheese
	black pepper (to taste)

Cream 4 tbsp. butter, mustard, shallots, garlic, vinegar and lemon peel. Set aside. Melt remaining butter and brown the bread crumbs. Set aside.

Boil water. Add broccoli and cauliflower. Return to boil for one minute. Scoop the florets out and add to the mustard butter, coating well. Cook the pasta until done. Drain. Mix hot pasta with mustard butter and veggie mixture. Serve topped with bread crumbs, parmesan cheese and pepper.

Mount Horeb Mustard Museum
Mustard Chex Mix

1/4 C.	margarine
1 1/2 tsp.	seasoning salt
2 1/2 tsp.	worcestershire sauce
2 tbsp.	mustard (a strong dijon or spicy mustard will do fine)
6 C.	mixed Chex cereal
1 C.	unsalted peanuts
1 C.	pretzels

Melt margarine and mix in mustard and seasonings. Stir into cereal, nuts and pretzels. Spread on cookie sheets. Bake 45 minutes at 250 degrees, stirring the mixture every 15 minutes. Allow to cool fully before eating.

Mount Horeb Mustard Museum
Zucchini Soup

3-4	medium zucchinis, chopped
1/2 C.	onion, chopped
1/4 C.	long grain rice
3 C.	chicken stock (homemade or canned)
1/2-1tsp.	curry powder
1 tsp.	dijon mustard
1/2-1C	yogurt (lowfat or nonfat)

Place zucchini, onion and rice in pot. Cover with chicken stock. Bring to boil, lower heat, and simmer 15 minutes or until tender.

Mash or puree in a blender (after allowing to cool slightly) until smooth. Add curry powder, mustard and yogurt. Gently heat for a hot soup or chill for cold soup.

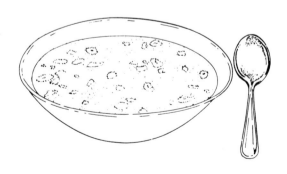

Mount Horeb Mustard Museum
Mustard Sorbet

1 1/4C.	water
1 1/2C.	sugar
5	yellow wax hot peppers, stems and seeds removed, chopped
1 lg.	orange, peeled and chopped
2 tbsp.	dark rum
3 tbsp.	mustard powder
4 tbsp.	fresh lemon juice
	- another 1/2 C. water-
3 tbsp.	light corn syrup

Combine 1 1/4 cup water with the sugar and heat until the sugar is dissolved. Bring to a boil, remove from the heat and cool to room temperature. Cool in the refrigerator for 2 hours. Puree the remaining ingredients with 1/2 cup water and also refrigerate for 2 hours. Stir the sugar mixture into the fruit. Pour into an ice cream maker and follow directions.

Jan Roberts-Dominguez, author of THE MUSTARD BOOK (Macmillan Publishing, 1993), writes and illustrates a nationally syndicated newspaper column, "Green Cuisine." She also writes and illustrates the "preserving" column for THE OREGONIAN in Portland. THE MUSTARD BOOK came about through Jan's personal experiences. Whenever she has written about how to make home-made designer mustards from scratch - using whole seeds rather than mustard powders - retailers have reported that whole seeds seemingly fly out of their bins in the bulk food departments.

The book also contains 40 watercolors, which Jan painted during the year she wrote the book and created the recipes. Jan holds a masters degree in home economics/foods & nutrition, has worked in a San Francisco test kitchen, taught, consulted, and is also the author and illustrator of two other cookbooks, GREEN CUISINE & OTHER COLORS OF HARVEST, and SANDWICH CUISINE, OREGON STYLE.

From THE MUSTARD BOOK
Muffulata Olive Relish

1/2 C.	coarsely chopped pimento-stuffed olives
1/2 C.	pitted black olives, coarsely chopped
1/4 C.	red onion, chopped
1/4 C.	fresh parsley, chopped
2 tbsp.	balsamic vinegar
1 tbsp.	garlic, minces
1 tsp.	capers, rinsed and drained
1/4 tsp.	dried oregano, crumbled
1/4 tsp.	freshly ground black pepper
1/4 C.	extra virgin olive oil

This is a marvelous concoction Jan uses to make the Muffulata Mustard. However, it's a wonderful mixture in its own right. Place it in a bowl alongside slices of a crusty baguette for a simple appetizer, spread it on a poor-boy sandwich that you've piled high with a selection of sliced meats, cheeses, tomato and pickled peppers.

Place the olives, onion, parsley, vinegar, garlic, capers, oregano, and pepper in a food processor. Pulse the mixture until the ingredients are finely chopped. Add the olive oil and continue processing until mixture is thoroughly chopped but not pureed. This will keep in the refrigerator for at least 2 weeks.

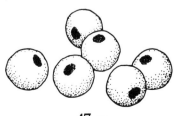

From THE MUSTARD BOOK
Muffulata Mustard

1/4 C.	yellow mustard seeds
1 C.	balsamic vinegar
1 C.	Muffulata Olive Relish
2 tsp.	salt

In a nonaluminum pot or jar, combine the mustard seeds and vinegar, cover and soak for 48 hours, adding vinegar if necessary to maintain enough liquid to cover the seeds.

Below are two options for completing this mustard. Jan's preference is for the textured version, in which the seeds are left whole, because the flavors are more vivid and the visual impact lovelier.

For a textured mustard (one with tender-yet-whole mustard seeds mingling with the zesty-flavored olive relish). Simply combine the soaked seeds with the relish and salt.

FOR A SMOOTHER-STYLE MUSTARD: Scrape the soaked seeds into a food processor, add the relish and salt and process until the mixture turns from liquid and seeds to a creamy mixture flecked with seeds and bits of olive. The process takes at least 3 to 4 minutes. You may need to add balsamic vinegar as necessary to create a nice creamy mustard keep in mind that it will thicken slightly upon standing. This is a mustard that can be enjoyed immediately. Makes about 3 1/2 cups.

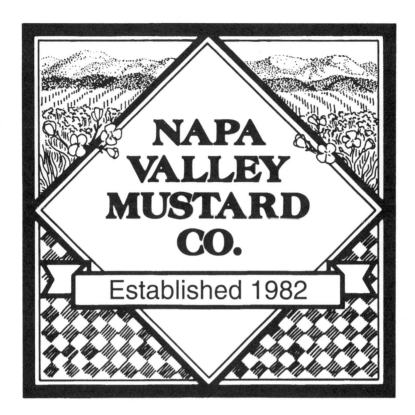

NAPA VALLEY MUSTARD CO.

Established 1982

The Wine Country's first mustard company was founded by three entrepreneurial Napa Valley women in 1982. Ann Grace, Ruthie Rydman and Susan Simpson were "inspired by Napa Valley's annual crop of beautiful mustard flowers, realizing how it reflected the heritage of this great wine region." Far more than just condiments, they believed that unique mustards are wonderful in marinades and glazes, and as just the right ingredient in a sauce, salad dressing and any dish that needs a little pizazz.

Napa Valley Mustard Company presently has four unique styles of mustard and have recently released a new product - Mustard Spiced Oil. Freshly press aromatic mustard oil is blended with Canola oil and olive oil which makes it both spicy and healthy. All products are made without preservatives or additives.

Napa Valley Mustard Company
Asparagus Mustard Pasta

1 ~ 16 oz.	dried spaghetti, cooked
2	bunches asparagus (2 lb. approx.)
3/4 C.	Mustard Spiced Oil
4 tsp.	lemon zest
	Cayenne pepper, salt to tast

Break off root end of asparagus spears, cut each spear into 3 pieces. Steam. Reserve tips. Puree (in blender) rest of asparagus and lemon zest in Mustard Spiced Oil. If necessary thin with lemon juice and/or pasta water. Add seasonings and toss cooked pasta in puree with reserved asparagus tip. Serves 8 people as side dish.

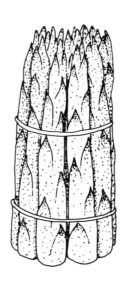

Napa Valley Mustard Company
Marinated Lamb Kabobs

1/2 C.	plain yogurt
1 tbsp.	California Hot Sweet Mustard
2 tbsp.	fresh mint, chopped
1 lg.	clove garlic, put through press
1 tbsp.	lemon juice
1/2 tsp.	salt
1/2 tsp.	fresh ground black pepper
3 lbs.	boneless leg of lamb, cut into 3/4 cubes

Stir lamb pieces into mixture of other ingredients and marinate in refrigerator overnight. Preheat grill or broiler until very hot. Skewer lamb cubes, reserving marinade. Place meat on grill or in broiler, turning skewers and basting with marinade from time to time for 8 to 10 minutes.

Napa Valley Mustard Company
Orange Ginger Mustard Stuffing

1/4 C.	butter
1/2 C.	yellow onion, chopped
1	garlic clove, chopped
1/2 C.	mushrooms, sliced
3 C.	cubed bread crumbs (packaged or fresh)
1/2 C.	tart apple, diced
1/4 C.	dried apricot, diced
1/4 C.	Orange Ginger Mustard
1/4 C.	pecans, chopped
1/2 tsp.	salt
1/8 tsp.	paprika

Melt butter and saute onion, garlic, mushrooms. Toss in bread crumbs and mix. Add rest of ingredients and moisten slightly with chicken broth. Makes about 4 1/2 cups. A great stuffing for a pork crowned roast, chicken or turkey.

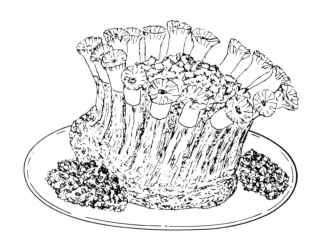

Napa Valley Tastes Collection is owned and operated by the Anestis' family. Since coming to the Napa Valley in 1969, they have owned and operated four successful restaurants.

In the early seventies the family was awarded the Plaque of World Famous Restaurants International. To this day, the family owns and operates a popular restaurant in the Napa Valley - Anestis'.

Their latest venture includes their Napa Valley Tastes Collection. Ernie Anesti created these products so people could experience the "tastes of the Napa Valley without ever leaving home." The essence of the wine country is reflected in each bottle of the Napa Valley Tastes' Collection. Their gourmet items include aromatic olive oil, an unforgettable salad dressing, marinaded olives, robust cheese, zesty seasonings and a gourmet mustard.

Napa Valley Tastes Collection
Tomato and Cucumber Salad

1 lb.	beefsteak or roma tomatoes, sliced
1	English cucumber (hot house), peeled and sliced
1 med.	red onion, sliced
3 oz.	Napa Valley Tastes Collection Virgin Olive Oil
2 oz.	balsamic vinegar
1 tsp.	Napa Valley Tastes Collection All Purpose Seasoning
1 tsp.	dried oregano

Place first 3 ingredients in salad bowl, mix dressing ingredients and pour over salad, sprinkle with oregano.

For extra flavor sprinkle with Feta Cheese and add Napa Valley Tastes Collection marinated Calamata Olives.

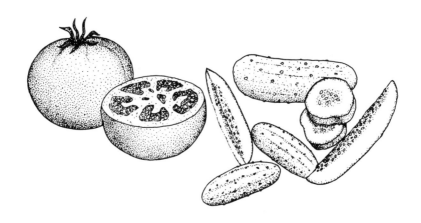

Napa Valley Tastes Collection
Roast Suckling Pig

30-40 lbs.   suckling pig
Napa Valley Tastes Collection
All Purpose Seasoning
Napa Valley Tastes Collection
Virgin Olive Oil
hot water
apple juice

Sprinkle pig throughout with Napa Valley Tastes All Purpose Seasoning, apply throughout with Napa Valley Tastes Virgin Olive Oil.

Place pig on a rack in a roasting pan in a 375 degree oven for approximately 2 1/2 - 3 1/2 hours until tender and golden brown, basting every 30 minutes with hot water and apple juice. Turn twice during cooking time. Serve with fried potatoes, lemon quarters and Napa Valley Tastes Mustard.

This recipe could also apply to a smaller portion of baby pig or 1-2 legs. Be sure to use a rack in roasting pan.

Napa Valley Tastes Collection
Caesar Dip

Place 1 cup of Napa Valley Tastes Caesar Salad dressing in a bowl in center of appetizer platter and surround with sticks of celery, carrots, broccoli, cauliflower or garlic croutons for dipping.

NapaValley WINE TRAIN®

Enjoy, relaxed elegance, artfully prepared cuisine and world class wines, aboard a lavishly restored 1915 Pullman dining and parlor cars whilst gently 'gliding' past world famous vineyards of the Napa Valley. Trains operate year round for lunch, brunch, or dinner.

Gourmet menus include appetizer, salad (or soup for the luncheon excursion), sorbet for the dinner excursion, entree and three to four accompanying side dishes, as well as daily dessert choices, coffee or tea. Full cocktail service is offered, in addition to almost 100 of the Valley's finest Vintners' selections. The meticulously restored dining cars are replete with etched glass, polished brass, fine rich fabrics, and imported Honduran mahogany. Guests are pampered with superb meals served with all the accoutrements of fine dining...damask linen, bone china, silver flatware and lead crystalware.

Napa Valley Wine Train
Lamb Loin in Mustard Seed Brioche

Mustard Seed Brioche

2 1/2 C.	bread flour
3 tbsp.	date sugar
1 tbsp.	dry milk
1/3 C.	butter
1 tsp.	salt
4 lg.	eggs, beaten
3/8 C.	water
1 pkg.	active dry yeast
2 tbsp.	mustard seed, crushed

Add all dry ingredients into the bread machine. Add the butter, eggs, water and yeast. Program the bread machine for the whole wheat dough mode.

At the end of the rising cycle, transfer the dough to an oiled bowl. Brush the top of the dough with oil and chill, tightly covered for 12 hours.

(This procedure can be done manually in a large mixing bowl and proofed in a warm area)

Lamb Loin in Mustard Seed Brioche con't:

2 lb.	lamb loin (denerver)
	cut a pocket into the top of the lamb loin and season the cavity with salt and white pepper
	spinach
2	cloves garlic
1 tbsp.	extra virgin olive oil

Saute crushed garlic and spinach in extra virgin olive oil until spinach is cooked. Let spinach cool and then press into a stainer to remove the liquid.

	flat bread
1 lb.	mustard seed brioche

To assemble place lamb on flat bread and stuff pocket with spinach. Roll tightly and set aside. Remove prepared mustard seed brioche from refrigerator, flour counterspace and roll out the dough 1/4 inch thick. Roll out large enough to completely cover up the lamb. Place lamb on the dough wrap around the lamb, coating the edges with egg wash. Brush additional egg wash on the surface of the loaf and bake in pre-heated 375 degree oven for one hour.

NORMAN BISHOP

California

DILL & GARLIC MUSTARD

Norman-Bishop's pleasantly creamy Dill & Garlic Mustard is pure dill heaven. Fantastic on fish, pasta and sandwiches!! There are six more wonderful Norman-Bishop condiments: Garlic Mustard, Smokey Sweet Mustard, Raspberry Mustard, Hot & Sweet Mustard Sauce, Garlic Mayonnaise and for spicy food lovers, Original Mexican Sauce.

It's not just something to spread on hot dogs. For a unique taste in preparing foods - add Norman-Bishop mustards. All products can be substituted for a mustard named in any receipe. The flavors can be interchanged according to taste and accompanying foods. Use Norman-Bishop mustards in salads, cream sauces, dips, meat dishes and etc.

Norman - Bishop
Low Calorie Orange, Mustard, and Yogurt Sauce or Salad Dressing

Particularly good with smoked chicken or turkey, or thin it down with extra orange, add some olive oil and use as a salad dressing.

1	sweet orange
2 tbsp. + 2 tsp.	Norman - Bishop Raspberry Mustard
1/2 C.	non-fat yogurt
	splash of balsamic vinegar
3-4	cardamon pods, seeds removed and crushed
	sprinkling of cinnamon (optional)

Very finely grate about a quarter of the orange zest into a bowl.

Squeeze the juice, stain and add with the mustard. Stir in the yogurt, add a dash of vinegar, then sprinkle the cardamom seeds and a touch of cinnamon. Chill lightly.

Norman - Bishop
Pork Chops & Apples
In Mustard Sauce

2 lbs.	green apples, peeled, cored and sliced thin
	salt & freshly ground pepper
4	thick pork loin chops, trimmed
1 tbsp.	butter or oil
1/4 C.	chicken broth
1 C.	heavy cream
1/3 C.	Norman-Bishop Smokey Mustard

Preheat oven to 400 degrees. Butter a 9 X 13 baking dish. Spread the apples over the bottom and bake for 15 minutes. Remove from heat and set aside.

Salt and pepper the pork chops to taste. Melt the butter or oil in a skillet and slowly brown the pork chops on each side. Remove the pork chops and place them over the apples. Heat the skillet over medium heat, add the broth and scrape the bottom, loosening and mixing the bits and juices remaining from the pork chops. Continue to stir, letting the mixture boil for a minute.

Put the cream and mustard in a small bowl and whisk until smooth. Add to the skillet with the broth mixture and bring just to a boil, stirring to blend. Pour over the top of the pork chops. Cover and bake 20 minutes.

OAK KNOLL INN

Driving through vineyards down tree-lined Oak Knoll
Avenue, it would be easy to miss the Oak Knoll Inn. A
stone building hidden behind a wall of cypress, it has one of
the most spectacular locations in Napa Valley. Walk through
the French-country style reception and dining rooms out to
the deck, and you're greeted with an unparalleled panorama.

Guest rooms overlook the surrounding 600 acres of
vineyards, aflame with wild mustard flowers during winter
months, and backed by Stag's Leap Mountain. A supply of
logs stands ready next to your marble-hearthed fireplace in
winter while the pool/spa beckon on warm summer days.

Stress from busy lives dissipates into the late-afternoon air
as convivial hosts Barbara Passino and John Kuhlmann offer
a delectable array of goodies for Wine and Cheese "hour."
Their years of international travel and Barbara's joy in
learning about other cultures through cooking with some
of the world's most eminent chefs are reflected in the menus--
served on pottery collected from all parts of the globe.

Oak Knoll Inn Aioli

Mustard is the key ingredient that makes this garlicky mayonnaise from Provence golden and delicious.

1	egg
4 lg.	cloves garlic, crushed
1 tsp.	dry mustard
1 tbsp.	dijon-style mustard
1/2 tsp.	salt
1/2 tsp.	freshly ground white pepper
2 tbsp.	fresh lemon juice
1 C.	Napa Valley olive oil

Place all ingredients EXCEPT OLIVE OIL in a blender. Cover and blend at medium speed until thoroughly combined. Remove the cover, and with the blender running, very slowly pour the olive oil in a stream into the mixture until it emulsifies and thickens. Chill. Serve with raw vegtables, fish or chicken.

Oak Knoll Inn
Broiled Fennel with Mustard

4 lg.	perfect fennel bulbs
2 tbsp.	Napa Valley olive oil
1/4 C.	dijon-style mustard
1 tbsp.	mustard seeds
1 tsp.	ground cumin
	salt and freshly ground pepper

Mix olive oil, mustard and mustard seeds. Trim the greens and stem from the fennel, leaving the bulb intact. Cut each lengthwise into 1/2 inch slices and spread on a broiler pan.

Sprinkle the slices with salt, pepper and cumin. Brush tops with half of the mustard mixture.

Broil about 6 inches from the flame for 5 minutes. Turn and brush with the remaining mustard and broil 5 minutes more.

Oak Knoll Inn Jalapeno Mustard

1/2 C.	mustard powder
1/2 C.	whole mustard seeds
1 tbsp.	ground cumin
3	jalapeno peppers, seeds and membrane removed
2	cloves garlic
1 tsp.	salt
1/3 C.	red wine vinegar
1/4 C.	water
1/4 C.	brown sugar

Puree all ingredients in a blender until mixed thoroughly. Makes approximately 1 cup. Keep tightly covered in a jar and refrigerate for two weeks to a month before using. It's good on sandwiches, and can also be mixed with Napa Valley olive oil to make a marinade for poultry, beef, lamb or pork using a ratio of 2 parts mustard to 3 parts oil.

Oak Knoll Inn Grill Lamb Steak

Marinate 2 pounds lamb "London Broil" in a mixture of the following:

1 tbsp.	mustard, coarse grained
3 tbsp.	fresh sage, minced (or 1tbsp. dried)
1 tsp.	lemon pepper
1/2 tsp.	cayenne pepper
1 tbsp.	grated onion
1/4 C.	Napa Valley olive oil
1/4 C.	balsamic vinegar
3 tbsp.	water

Marinate the lamb at least 4 hours, preferable overnight, turning occasionally. Grill 5 minutes per side for medium rare, basting with the marinade.

Oakwood
A Bed & Breakfast Inn

Oakwood, secluded and quiet, fits almost everyone's idea of an ideal vacation retreat. Oakwood is located in Calistoga, a small town in the uppermost portion of this world-famous grape growing area.

The charm of the wine country is evident everywhere you look and Oakwood is no exception. Accommodations consist of two separate, intimate cottages, each decorated to create their own individual private mood. Nearby are infinite things to see and do. Take the waters at the Spas of Calistoga with their mud & mineral baths. Perhaps a bicycle tour through our beautiful countryside on well-marked paths. You might want to take to the air in a sail-plane or balloon, and then treat yourself to a memorable meal at one of Calistoga's notable restaurants. And...the list goes on and on...

Oakwood
A Bed & Breakfast Inn
Cornish Game Hens Dijonnaise

2	Cornish game hens split in two backbone removed
2 oz.	butter
3/4 C.	chicken stock
1 tbsp.	flour
	grated rind (no white) and juice of 2 oranges
1 tbsp.	Dijon mustard or Napa Valley Mustard
2 tbsp.	whipping cream
	parsley to garnish

Heat a large flame proof casserole, melt half of the butter. Salt and pepper game hens, place skin side down saute until golden brown, turn and saute other side, 3 to 4 minutes per side. Add chicken stock, cover and cook in a 350 degree oven until tender, approx. 20 to 30 minutes.

Remove from pan arrange game hen skin side up for grilling in a separate ovenproof dish.

Blend flour into remaining butter, then add to the juices in the casserole. Over medium heat stir until boiling, strain and keep warm.

Sprinkle hens with orange juice, grill until golden brown and crisp. Add mustard and orange rind to sauce, check for seasoning, heat, add cream. Do not boil. Pour sauce around the game hens and garnish with parsley.

Oakwood
A Bed & Breakfast Inn
Herbed Vinaigrette

1 C.	Extra Virgin Olive Oil
1/3 C.	Balsamic Vinegar
2 tbsp.	Matthews Garlic & Horseradish Mustard
1/2 tsp.	sugar
1 tsp.	salt
1 tsp.	ground black pepper
2 tbsp.	chopped shallots
2 tbsp.	chopped parsley
2 tbsp.	chopped tarragon

Combine all ingredients in a bowl and mix well, allow to stand 4 to 5 hours before use.

TARRAGON

The Old World Inn

"A holiday of romance and gourmet delights" appropriately describes a stay at the Old World Inn. This charming 1906 Victorian features Scandinavian country decor and unparalleled food service. Warm pastel colors brightly decorate the inn's interior and an extensive array of stencilled artwork and sayings adorn the walls. Each room is uniquely decorated and features either a queen or king size bed and private bath. For romance, choose a room with a canopy bed, skylights or sunken spa tub or simply enjoy an evening dip under the stars in the outdoor spa.

Expect to be spoiled with home-baked delights from morning till night. Savor afternoon tea and cookies when you arrive or retreat to your room where complimentary wine awaits you. In the evening unwind at the wine and cheese social or be enticed with a chocolate lover's dessert buffet. In the morning you'll awaken to the smell of fresh brewed coffee and a gourmet breakfast.

Old World Inn
Asparagus Frittata

12 oz.	grated cheddar cheese
12 oz.	cooked asparagus
8 oz.	sour cream
6	eggs
1 tbsp.	Napa Valley Mustard Company California Hot Sweet Mustard
2 tbsp.	chives, chopped
1/4 tsp.	dill
1/4 C.	parsley

Prepare 9" round pan. Cover bottom with grated cheese. Place asparagus over cheese. Blend together sour cream, eggs, mustard, chopped chives, dill and parsley. Pour over cheese and asparagus. Bake in 350 degree oven for 25 to 30 minutes or until set. Cool 10 minutes before cutting.

MEXICAN
Bar & Grill

Pacifico is a favorite gathering place for both locals and tourists. Whether on a cold, rainy night or a steamy afternoon, the decor is inviting and creates a warm fun-filled atmosphere. Tile floors, brick, rock and adobe walls, punctuated by lush tropical plants and a unique collection of cacti are reminiscent of a true Mexican bar and grill.

Their cuisine is unique and exciting, featuring such items as red hot Chimayo chile sauce covering the Carnitas las Cruces, and the Mulato Hollandaise, adding an unsurpassed dimension to the Eggs Benedict. Fresh salsa served at every table with toasted tortillas chips and fresh roasted chiles make these meals plentiful. The grill provides delicately prepared fish and meats. Any meal is a memorable experience complemented by a delicious hand shaken Margarita or a cold Mexican beer, and served by friendly, efficient staff.

Pacifico Mexican Bar & Grill
Carnitas Tacos

5 lb.	Pork butts
1/4 C.	coriander, ground
1/4 C.	fresh black pepper
1/4 C.	salt
1 tbsp.	dry mustard
1 lg.	garlic head, halved
1 lg.	onion, quartered
1 lg.	orange, quartered
2 lb.	onion, chopped and sauteed
1 lb.	fresh cilantro, chopped
	corn tortillas

Put pork in deep pan. Cover the meat with all ingredients EXCEPT SAUTEED ONIONS AND CILANTRO. Cover with aluminum foil and cook in a 450 degree oven for 2 hours or until meat is very tender. Remove meat from oven and when cool enough, shred the meat and combine with sauted onions and cilantro.

Steam or grill corn tortillas, place meat in tortilla, fold and serve.

Pairs

Eloquence in Food and Wine

Chef de Cuisine, Craig Schauffel and Event Coordinator, Anne Pentland began their association running the hospitality department for a local winery. Working within a winery gave them the ability to understand the dynamic qualities of wine, and sharpened their awareness of the balance between food and wine. Pairs; Eloquence in Food and Wine was begun from their desire to offer to the many local wineries this same special attention to food and wine pairing.

Pairs is dedicated to providing the highest quality menus with specific consideration for the wines to be served. They create custom menus continually to reflect the freshest seasonally available ingredients. Attention to detail, from the arrangement of the food on the plate, with fine china and linen, to superlative service, is their standard.

Pairs; Eloquence in Food & Wine
Lemon Fried Calamari
with Crispy Celery Root
and Tarragon Mustard Aioli

1 lb.	small calamari, cleaned
1	head of celery root, peeled, sliced by quarters and sliced thinly
2 ea.	lemons, sliced paper thin
3 C.	flour
8 C.	oil, for deep frying

Slice calamari tubes into small rings, and leave tentacles whole. Heat deep fat fryer with oil to 350 degrees. Coat calamari evenly with salt and pepper, then lightly flour and fry 1 to 2 minutes until crisp and golden brown. Season with salt and pepper. Serve with tarragon mustard aioli.

Pairs; Eloquence in Food and Wine
Tarragon Mustard Aioli

1	russet potato, boiled until tender, riced and cooled
3	egg yolks
1-2	cloves garlic, minced
1 tbsp.	dijon mustard
1	lemon, juiced
1 tbsp.	tarragon, chopped
	salt and pepper
1 pt.	corn oil

Place riced potato in a bowl with egg yolk, garlic, mustard, lemon juice, tarragon, and combine with wire wisk. Slowly infuse the corn oil into the potato mixture using cold water to thin as necessary until all the oil is incorporated. Adjust consistency with cold water and season with salt and pepper.

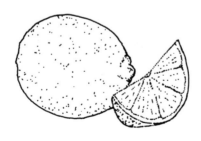

Pairs Parkside Cafe
Citrus Mustard Baked Salmon with Caraway Cabbage and Fennel Slaw

4	Salmon Filets, 6-8 oz. skinned
8 oz.	citrus mustard (or dijon with juice of one lemon)
	salt and pepper

Coat salmon filets with salt and pepper evenly, then coat with citrus mustard. Place on an oiled sheet tray and bake at 350 degrees in oven for 8 to 10 minutes until done. Serve with caraway cabbage and fennel slaw.

Pairs Parkside Cafe
Caraway Cabbage and Fennel Slaw

1 lg.	yellow onion, thinly sliced
1 sm.	green cabbage, shredded
2 heads	fennel, thinly sliced
1 tbsp.	caraway
2 oz.	bacon fat or corn oil
	salt and pepper

In a large sauté pan heat oil and sauté onions until translucent. Add cabbage and fennel and cook until tender. Add caraway, cook for 5 minutes and season with salt and pepper.

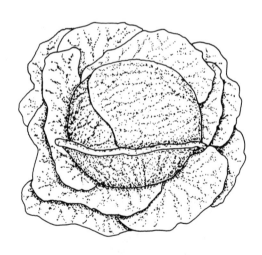

PR⬤VISI⬤NS

Purveyors of specialty foods
from the wine country and beyond

Founded by wine country residents Susan McWilliams, Jamie Morningstar and Ken Hearnsberger, PROVISIONS specializes in locally-produced wine country specialty foods, marketing them nationwide through a direct mail catalog.

From fruity olive oils and fragrant Napa Valley herbs to zesty olive salsas, PROVISIONS captures the sunny flavors that have made wine country cuisine as famous as the region's wines. Drawing on extensive food and wine experience, the partners select foods for their superb quality, enhancing the catalog with recipes by Morningstar, a professional chef. PROVISIONS has introduced two products under its own colorful label: A richly-flavored Wild Mushroom Risotto and savory Polenta with Sun-Dried Tomatoes.

PROVISIONS
Mustard-Spiced Polenta Toasts

1 pkg.   Provisions Polenta with Tomatoes
Napa Valley Mustard Co.
Mustard Spiced Oil

Prepare polenta according to directions on package and pour into a greased 9" bread pan to cool. Refrigerate several hours or overnight. Preheat oven to 400 degrees. Slice polenta into 1/4" slices and cut each slice in half.

Lightly oil baking sheet with mustard spiced oil. Place polenta slices on pan and brush tops with mustard spiced oil. Bake until golden brown - approximately 10 to 15 minutes. Serve as hors d'oeuvres with a variety of toppings such as:

-smoked salmon and sour cream with 1 tsp. dijon-style mustard and snipped chives;

-grated Mozzarella cheese, broil until cheese melts, then top with olive salsa or roasted peppers;

-vine-ripe tomatoes, chopped and combined with crushed garlic, fresh basil, mustard oil and salt to taste.

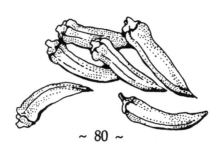

J.W. RAYE & Co. Inc.

In 1903, when the Coast of Maine bristled with canneries, wharfs and schooners, Raye's Mustard Mill was founded by John Wesley Raye. The son of a sea captain, "J.W." saw business opportunities ashore in producing mustard which could be shipped by the barrel from the port of Eastport. "Wes" set up a classic 19th century mustard mill replete with wooden barrels, aging tank and a cooper's shop. The heart of the mill is the series of rare hand-cut granite grindstones, each weighing about one ton, which grind the world's finest aromatic seeds and true spices into a variety of mustard blends.

In 1990, Nancy Raye, J.W.'s grand-daughter returned from Northern California to manage the family legacy. Today Raye's Mill, the country's last stone mustard mill in operation, is where the quality of yesteryear is kept alive in the taste of today's fine mustards.

Raye's Three-Mustard Potato Salad

3 lb.	small red potatoes
1 C.	mayonnaise
1 tbsp.	Raye's Traditional mustard (brown, any style)
1 tbsp.	Raye's Hot & Spicy mustard (yellow/grain, any style)
1 tbsp.	fresh lemon juice
1 tbsp. + 1 tsp.	extra virgin olive oil
1 tbsp. + 1 tsp.	yellow mustard seeds
	salt and freshly ground pepper

Cook potatoes in salted water until tender. Drain, cool, peel (or not) and cut into 1/2" chunks. Combine mayonnaise, mustards and lemon juice. Mix potatoes and mustard dressing. Set aside. Using a small skillet, combine mustard seeds and olive oil. Cover and cook over moderate heat until the seeds start to pop (1-2 minutes). Remove from heat and keep shaking covered skillet until popping stops. Scrape seeds and oil onto salad and fold gently to mix. Season to taste with salt and pepper. Cover and refrigerate. Can be made up to two days in advance.

Scarlett's Country Inn

An intimate retreat tucked away in a small canyon, Scarlett's Country Inn has three exquisitely appointed suites set in the quiet mood of green lawns and tall pines overlooking the vineyards on the edge of the forest. All have private entrances, private bathrooms, queen beds and air conditioning. One suite has a fireplace and both suites have fold out couches in the living rooms for an extra person or child.

Scarlett pampers you with special soaps, fresh flowers, robes in the closet and phones in your room if you wish. Enjoy a delicious breakfast served on the deck under the apple trees or in your own cozy sitting room. Complimentary refreshments are served in the afternoon and innkeepers are happy to help you with all your activity planning. This 1890 country farmhouse is located just minutes from fine restaurants, wineries, and spas. Children are welcome at no extra charge.

Scarlett's Mustard Chicken

6	skinned chicken breasts
1/2 C.	teriyake sauce
2 tbsp.	Napa Valley Mustard Co. Hot Sweet Mustard
2 tbsp.	Miss Scarlett's Ginger Pear Jelly
1	onion
6	small new potatoes
6	carrots

Spray baking dish lightly with oil. Arrange chicken breasts, meat side up, in bottom of baking dish. Pour teriyake sauce over breasts. Spread each breast with mustard. Dot Ginger Pear Jelly on each breast. Slice onion and lay over chicken. Cut potatoes and carrots into small pieces and place in between chicken. If desired, pour in a small amount of wine. Bake covered in a 425 degree oven for about 45 minutes or until vegetables are soft.

Scarlett's Mustard Dressing

2 tbsp.	red wine vinegar
2 tbsp.	Napa Valley Mustard Co. California Hot Sweet Mustard
2 C.	extra virgin cold press olive oil

Pour vinegar into a blender, add mustard and blend a few seconds. Slowly add olive oil in a continuous stream through the top of the blender while it is running. Mixture should thicken. Increase blender speed if mixture stops blending before you have added all of the oil. Enjoy on all your salads or cold vegetables.

SCOTT

COURTYARD

Scott Courtyard makes you feel as though you're in a Mediterranean villa with latticed garden pathways to private suites. All rooms have their own entrances, queen beds and private baths. The poolside social room, has been described as romantic "tropical art deco". Enjoy a full breakfast in our Bistro Style Kitchen. Just two blocks from historic Lincoln Avenue, you are close to fine dining, excellent shops, the gliderport, and Calistoga's world famous Spas.

Three of the six suites have fireplaces and three private bungalows are equipped with kitchens. In the early evening refreshments are served in the social room, with its 29 foot vaulted ceiling and fireplace. A separate television room is available for your convenience.

Scott Courtyard
Sliced Eggs with Mustard Sauce

6	hard boiled eggs
6 tbsp.	mayonnaise
2 tbsp.	dijon mustard
2 tsp.	olive oil
1 clove	garlic, crushed
1/2 tsp.	dill
1 tbsp.	capers
6	slices ham, thin sliced

Cut ham into 2 inch squares. Horizontally cut eggs with egg slicer. Layer ham and eggs. Prepare remaining mixture (except capers) and mix thoroughly. Let stand 10 minutes.

Put mustard mixture on eggs and sprinkle with capers. Serves six as appetizers or brunch.

DILL

SHOWLEY'S
AT MIRAMONTE

Located one block east of Main Street in central St. Helena, this charming restaurant serves California cuisine with strong French and Italian influences. From pates to ice creams, everything is made in-house with the finest ingredients. The menu changes daily for both lunch and dinner. The Showley's take advantage of the region's domesticated wild game, goat cheeses, fields of local greens and vegetables, and wild mushrooms.

The 1858 building has a restful and gracious feeling that restores the weary traveler and excites the culinary adventurer. In the warmer weather the garden courtyard is "the place" in the Napa Valley where the century old fig tree canopies the diners. The Wine Spectator award winning wine list is extensive, concentrating on California wines and offering one of the largest selections of Pinot Noir in the Napa Valley. Showley's is open for lunch and dinner Tuesday through Sunday.

Showley's Chicken Breast
with Lemon Mustard Sauce

8	chicken breasts, boned and skinless
1 C.	dijon mustard
1/4 C.	olive oil
2 tbsp.	mustard, whole grained
2	lemons, juiced
1 C.	whipping cream

In a large stainless steel bowl whisk together 1/2 cup of the dijon mustard and olive oil until emulsified. Place the chicken breasts in the mixture and toss until well coated. Let marinate at least one hour or overnight.

Heat the BBQ or charbroiler until hot, grill the chicken breasts on both sides. Or you may saute them in a skillet.

Meanwhile, in a sauce pan mix the rest of the ingredients together and heat until hot.

Mirror the sauce on the plate and place the cooked chicken breast on top and serve.

Showley's Country Potato Salad

3 lbs.	new potatoes
2 C.	mustard, whole grained
1/2 C.	olive oil
1	bunch parsley, finely chopped

Heat 2 quarts of water to a boil. Add 1/4 cup of salt and add potatoes. Cook for 25-35 minutes until a knife pierces the potato with no resistance. Drain the water and let the potatoes cool. Once cool, cut into quarters. Mix together the mustard and olive oil until emulsified. Add to the potatoes and mix together well. Add parsley and serve.

Showley's
Veal Sweetbreads with Shallot, Mushrooms & Whole Grain Mustard Sauce

2-3 lb.	veal sweetbreads
1/2 C.	white wine vinegar
1 lb.	white mushrooms, cut into quarters
1/2 lb.	peeled and sliced shallots
1/4 C.	mustard, whole grained
2 tbsp.	melted butter
1/2 C.	madeira wine
1/2 C.	chicken or veal demiglace
1	bunch Italian parsley, finely chopped

Showley's
Veal Sweetbreads with Shallot, Mushrooms & Whole Grain Mustard Sauce

To prepare sweetbreads: Heat 2 quarts of water to a boil. Add 2 tbsp. salt and 1/2 cups vinegar. While heating soak the sweetbreads in cold water changing the water until clear. Add the sweetbreads to the hot water and bring back to a boil. Let simmer for 12 minutes. Remove the sweetbreads from the water and place between two plates or two cookie sheets. Weigh down with a heavy skillet and let cool. This will remove the bitterness and compress the sweetbreads to facilitate slicing. Once cool remove any membranes and fat from the outside of the sweetbread lobes. Then slice in half horizontally. Set aside.

In a large skillet heat the butter until hot but not smoking. Add the sweetbreads and saute until colored. Flip them over and add the mushrooms, shallots and mustard, saute for 1 minute then add the madeira and demiglace. Continue to cook until the sauce begins to thicken. Remove the sweetbread to serving plate and continue to heat the sauce until thick. Add chopped parsley and pour over the sweetbreads.

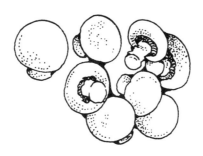

Silver Rose Inn

—HOT SPRINGS—

Located on a peaceful 20 acre estate, just minutes from Calistoga, in the Napa Valley, this country inn offers privacy and relaxation among elegant surroundings. From the gathering room with its huge stone fireplace and cozy reading nooks inside to the expansive terraces and rose gardens outside. In addition, a charming rock garden with a gentle waterfall, fed by hot springs, cascades down into the pool, jacuzzi and large deck area below.

The Inn has nine guest rooms...each has a private bath, king or queen sized bed, sitting area and beautiful mountain and vineyard views. Every room is tastefully decorated and was carefully designed around a special theme. Many rooms offer fireplaces, whirlpool tubs and private balconies. Enjoy Silver Rose Cellars Chardonnay and Cabernet Sauvignon with cheese and crackers every afternoon and complimentary breakfast each morning.

Silver Rose Inn
Poached Chicken Breasts in
Orange Ginger Mustard Sauce

4	chicken breasts (no bones or skin)
4 tsp.	orange ginger mustard
4 tbsp.	concentrated orange juice
1/3 C.	diluted orange juice
8	slices fresh ginger

Place chicken breasts on a large sheet of foil. Rub each breast with 1 tsp. orange ginger mustard. Pour 1 tbsp. concentrated orange juice over each breast. Pour 1/3 C. diluted orange juice over chicken. Place 2 slices of fresh ginger on each breast. Fold foil like an envelope to keep in all the juices. Bake in a 350 degree oven for 45 minutes. Serve over wild rice.

SOO YUAN

The first Soo Yuan restaurant opened in 1974, in Taipei, Taiwan. When the family immigrated to the United States, a brother remained behind to manage that facility. "Soo Yuan" translated means "nice place" or "nice garden." Their chosen decor represents the beautiful lakes and flowers found in the "Soo" province in Mainland China. The owners, Shan and Meiling Fang, have been involved in preparing and serving Chinese food for more than 15 years and have selected these menu items from hundreds of Chinese dishes.

Soo Yuan I, located in Calistoga, continues to serve our up-valley patrons seven days a week. Soo Yuan II, their second location in the Napa Valley is in the town of Napa. Serving "authentic" Mandarin, Szechuan or Hunan style Chinese dinners, the Fangs often mingle with their guests making recommendations to make their dining experience even more enjoyable.

Soo Yuan Restaurant
Eggroll

Filling:

4 oz.	ground pork
8 lb.	cabbage, shredded
1	onion, sliced
4 oz.	bamboo shoots, sliced
4 oz.	bean sprouts
32	eggroll skins

Dressing:

1 tbsp.	oil
2 tbsp.	soy sauce
1 tsp.	sugar
1 tsp.	chicken broth granules
1 tsp.	white pepper
1 tbsp.	cooking wine
1 tbsp.	sesame oil

Put oil in a wok; add ground pork; stir fry pork until it is well done. Add cabbage, onion, bamboo shoots and bean sprouts. Add soy sauce, sugar, chicken broth and white pepper while stir frying the vegetables. Cook until all the vegetables are well done (soft). Splash the sesame oil on the top. Take out everything from the wok and put in colander. Drain, then make eggroll.

THE TWO
VIRGINS[tm]

The Two Virgins was founded in 1982, a result of owner Pauline Sortor's lifelong interest in the "relishes and savouries" of her native home - England. Opening in Ghirardelli Square, San Francisco in 1983 and in 1989 at the Pavilion, San Jose, the business has become a thriving gourmet foods and gift store with the core TWO VIRGINS mustards, chutneys, sauces and other specialties at the heart of the business.

A personalized gift basket division serves corporate clients in the Silicon Valley and a mail order regularly delivers TWO VIRGINS products to customers across the United States. In addition, a new catering division was debuted in late 1993 in time for the busy holiday season. Because TWO VIRGINS products are not offered wholesale, they are available only at the two existing outlets and, of course by phone, mail or fax order.

THE TWO VIRGINS
Chicken Cantata

4	boneless chicken breasts
	flour to dredge,
	salt and pepper to taste
2 tbsp.	butter
1/3 C.	white wine or brandy
3 tbsp.	TWO VIRGINS CRANBERRY CANTATA

In a thick skillet over medium heat, melt butter. Flatten chicken breasts by pounding lightly with the rim of a heavy saucer. Dredge in seasoned flour and, when butter is sizzling, saute on each side until browned and cooked through. Remove to serving dish and keep warm.

To the pan juices, add the wine or brandy, lowering heat and using wooden spatula to incorporate all the brown bits into the liquid. When liquid is thickened and slightly reduced, add the cranberry Cantata and stir until blended. Remove from heat. Spoon over chicken breasts. Serve with baked yams and brussel sprouts and pass a separate dish of Cranberry Cantata.

THE TWO VIRGINS
Kidney Bean and Cabbage Slaw

1 ~ 14oz.	can red kidney beans, drained
1/4 C.	white wine vinegar
1/2 C.	Maiden's Breath Mustard
3/4 C.	vegetable oil
2-3 lb.	cabbage, shredded
6	carrots, shredded
1/2 C.	scallion, minced
2	cloves garlic, minced

In a blender combine wine vinegar, Maiden's Breath Mustard and add, in a thin stream, while blending, the vegetable oil. When dressing is emulsified, mix beans, cabbage, carrots, scallions and garlic together in a bowl, pour over dressing, remix, add salt and cracked pepper to taste.

THE TWO VIRGINS
Dragon Baked Potatoes

2 lb.	small red potatoes
1 tbsp.	olive oil
1 tbsp.	salt
2-3 tbsp.	The Two Virgins Dragon's Breath Mustard

Wash potatoes, dry, rub skins with olive oil until well coated. Cut in half (if larger potatoes, cut into quarters). Sprinkle lavishly with salt (don't worry, much of the salt will "sweat off") Allow potatoes to sit on slotted oven rack for 10 to 15 minutes so that the salt can draw out some of the moisture.

Using slotted oven rack, not a cookie sheet or baking pan, roast potatoes in a 475 degree oven for 20 minutes until fork tender. Turn heat up to 500 degrees and roast another 5 to 10 minutes until potatoes are puffed and golden.

Turn potatoes into serving bowl with 2-3 tbsp. Dragon's Breath Mustard, mix until well coated.

THE TWO VIRGINS
Devine Deviled Eggs

1	doz.	eggs
1/2	C.	mayonnaise
1/2	C.	sour cream
2	tbsp.	curry powder
1/2	tsp.	salt
1/2	jar	The Two Virgins Charlie's Chutney small amount of red and green peppers for garnish

Bring eggs to boil, cook for 8 to 10 minutes, plunge in cold water to cool. Peel and slice in half the long way, removing yolk to bowl. Add to yolks the mayonnaise and sour cream (low fat or both okay) mash thoroughly, add the curry powder and salt, mix again, fold in the Charlie's Chutney. Fill the egg whites with the mixture and garnish with small strips of red and green peppers.

Wilson's Black Mustard has a uniqueness in flavor that puts it in a category all of its own. Often referred to as "Poor man's Caviar", be sure to taste its elegance...straight from the jar!

Experience the difference when this condiment is spread lightly over smoked salmon or pork chops. Black Mustard may also be used as a marinate in creating your own culinary masterpiece. To give that special occasion a look of elegance, with taste to match, remember Wilson's Black Mustard, when serving champagne and hor d'oeuvres.

Simply add a little olive oil to taste, and you will find Black Mustard great over a garden salad. Wilson's Black Mustard may be purchased at your local Specialty Food Store, or Cost Plus Imports throughout the West Coast.

Wilson's Black Mustard
Muffin Snack

2 tbsp.	Wilson's Black Mustard
1 tbsp.	French dressing
4 oz.	Cream cheese
2	English Muffins split in halves

Combine Wilson's Black Mustard with French dressing. Toast English Muffins. Spread with cream cheese and mustard mixture. Its fast, easy and delicious!

Wilson's Red Mustard
Scrambled Eggs

2 tbsp.	Wilson's Red Mustard
6	eggs
2 tsp.	chives chopped
2 tbsp.	finely grated parmesan cheese
1 tbsp.	butter

Beat eggs with Wilson's Red Mustard. Melt butter in frying pan over medium heat, add eggs and scramble to desired consistency. Serve topped with chives and parmesan cheese.

List of Cookbook Participants

Aidells Sausage Company
1575 Minnesota St.
San Francisco, CA 94107
415/285~6660; Fax 415-285-1897

All Seasons Cafe & Catering
1400 Lincoln Ave.
Calistoga, CA 94515
707/942~9111

Auberge du Soleil
180 Rutherford Hill Road
Rutherford, CA 94573
707/962~1211

Big Daddy's at the Calistoga Gliderport
1522 Lincoln Ave.
Calistoga, CA 94515
707/942~9503

Brava Terrace
3010 St. Helena Hwy.
St. Helena, CA 94574
707/963~9300; Fax 707/963~9581

Calistoga Inn
1250 Lincoln Ave.
Calistoga, CA 94515
707/942-4101

Candlelight Inn
1045 Easum Drive
Napa, CA 94558
707/257~3717

Checkers Restaurant
    1414 Lincoln Ave.
    Calistoga, CA 94515
    707/942~9300

Cinnamon Bear Bed & Breakfast
    1407 Kearney St.
    St. Helena, CA 94574
    707/433~6991

East Shore Specialty Foods
    N44W32882 Watertown Plank Rd.
    P.O. Box 138
    Nashotah, WI 53058
    414/367-8988; Fax 414/367~9081

Foothill House Bed & Breakfast
    3037 Foothill Blvd.
    Calistoga, CA 94515
    707/942-6933

Forest Manor Bed & Breakfast
    415 Cold Springs Rd.
    Angwin, CA 94508
    707/965~3538

Hennessey House Bed & Breakfast
    1727 Main St.
    Napa, CA 94559
    707/226~3774

La Chaumiere a country inn
    1301 Cedar St.
    Calistoga, CA 94515
    707/942~5139; 800/474~6800

Lord Derby Arms English Pub
1923 Lake Street
Calistoga, CA 94515
707/942~9155

Mendocino Mustard Incorporated
1260 North Main Street
Fort Bragg, CA 95437
707/964~2250

The Mount Horeb Mustard Museum
P. O. Box 468
109 East Main Street
Mount Horeb, WI 53572
608/437~3986

The Mustard Book
Jan-Roberts-Dominguez
MacMillan Publishing Co.
866 Third Avenue
New York, NY 10022
503/752~7060

Napa Valley Mustard Company
P.O. Box 125
Oakville, CA 94562
707/944~8330

Napa Valley Tastes
P.O. Box 3064
6518 Washington St.
Yountville, CA 94599
1-800/972~7837; Fax 707/944~8613

Napa Valley Wine Train
1275 McKinstrey Street
Napa, CA 94559
707/253~2160

Norman Bishop Mustard Company
P.O. Box 2451
San Jose, CA 98109
408/292~1089; Fax 408/295~0333

Oak Knoll Inn
2200 E. Oak Knoll Ave.
Napa Valley, 94558
707/255~2200

Oakwood A Bed & Breakfast Inn
1503 Lake Street
Calistoga, CA 94515
707/942~5381

The Old World Inn
1301 Jefferson St.
Napa, CA 04559
707/257~0112

Pacifico Mexican Bar & Grill
1237 Lincoln Ave.
Calistoga, CA 94515
707/942~4400

Pairs; Eloquence in Food & Wine
1812 Michael Way
Calistoga, CA 94515
707/942~5483

Pairs Parkside Cafe
1420 Main Street
St. Helena, CA 94574
707/963~7566

Provisions
P.O. Box 3371
Yountville, CA 94599
800/789~PROV

Raye's Mustard Mill
P.O. Box 2
Eastport, ME 04631
207/853~4451

Scarlett's Country Inn
3918 Silverado Trail, N.
Calistoga, CA 94515
707/942~6669

Scott Courtyard
1443 2nd St.
Calistoga, CA 94515

Showley's At Miramonte
1327 Railroad Ave.
St. Helena, CA 94574
707/963~ 8864

Silver Rose Inn
351 Rosedale Rd.
Calistoga, CA 94515
707/942~9581

Soo Yuan I
1354 Lincoln Ave.
Calistoga, CA 94515
707/942~9404

Soo Yuan II
1144 Jordan Lane
Napa, CA 94558
707/224~8788

The Two Virgins
900 North Point
San Francisco, CA 94109
415/775~7589

Wilson's English Mustard
Imported by Cal-Imports
P.O. Box 1985
Tracy, CA 95378
209/832-5566; Fax 209/832~5569

Your own
Mustard Magic
recipes & notes

CALISTOGA

NATURAL BEVERAGES

THE
PERFECT
ACCOMPANIMENT
TO FINE
FOOD

PURE REFRESHMENT FROM THE NAPA VALLEY

CALISTOGA PRESS

SPECIALIZING IN WINE LABELS

OUR RECIPE TO SERVE YOU BETTER:

KNOWLEDGABLE PERSONNEL,
DEPENDABLE, ON-TIME DELIVERIES.
COURTEOUS SERVICE

1401 TUBBS LANE,CALISTOGA ,CA.

707-942-6033

Napa Valley Mustard Festival Cookbook
Order Form

Please send_____ copies of The Napa Valley Mustard Festival Cookbook at $11.95.

Add $ 2.50 for postage and handling for each book ordered.

Enclosed is my check for _____

Name _____

Address _____

City _____ State_____ Zip_____

This is a gift. Send directly to:

Name _____

Address _____

City _____ State_____ Zip_____

Books may be autographed upon request!

Mail to: Napa Valley Mustard Celebraton
P.O. Box 495
Calistoga, CA 94515